LALITAMBA

the first one

Printed in accordance with
the Sustainable Forestry Initiative.

Third Edition

First published online in 2005
with special thanks to Hari Mulukutla

ISBN 978-09778633-1-0
ISSN 1930-0662

The name for the journal was inspired by a devotional song, "Lalitamba, Lalitamba," sung on a tour through India with Sri Mata Amritanandamayi Devi. In early 2004, we traveled through the country in an effort to alleviate the suffering that comes with poverty, illness, and loss of hope. The journal was founded in November of 2004 by Swamini Sri Lalitambika Devi.

The name Lalitamba means Divine Mother. In India, the Divine Mother is thought of as *jagado dharini,* or She who supports the universe. The journal *Lalitamba* publishes writings and artwork that explore meaning, relationship, and truth. It is a journal of modern mysticism.

Submission Guidelines: Please submit up to five poems or one work of prose per envelope. Work should be previously unpublished. Please include SASE and contact information, including email address. Please address all correspondence to:

Lalitamba
P.O. Box 131
Planetarium Station
New York, NY 10024

Subscriptions are $12 for one annual issue, plus $4.50 postage and handling. We are a 501(c)(3) nonprofit organization serving hospitals, prisons, and shelters.

www.lalitamba.org

Lalitamba is affiliated with Refuge, a women's shelter in New York City.

www.threejewelsrefuge.org

TABLE OF CONTENTS

Fiction

Poetry

Samantha Holloway

Melinda Miller's Laugh

The day Melinda Miller broke through the depression that had gripped her for the three years since her husband's departure was a day everyone would remember.

She woke, suddenly and completely, on the night of the full moon, when the whole world was clothed in liquid silver. Melinda sat up in bed, and her eyes, dark with sadness and self-loathing, took in the light. They drank it in until they were bright and shining, two silver coins in her sad-but-softening face.

When her eyes could hold no more light, it began to spill across her face, pouring out over her body to form a shimmering path before her. Melinda followed it — hesitantly at first, then with more confidence. The trail of light led her into the hallway, down the stairs, and through the main rooms of the house. She followed it, drifting like a ghost, the light falling from her eyes, glinting off of small treasures, the trinkets and debris of her life, making them real to her for the first time in years.

The path led her out the back door to the porch. There, it pooled around the base of a potted plant she had thought long dead. Melinda knelt before it, her eyes glowing and her nightgown white. She touched one of the brittle leaves. Her light slid over the plant like water, and where it touched, the brown turned green.

She looked closely and saw that the plant had begun to bud with small flowers, the color of heart's blood spilled long ago. As she watched, the red blossom nearest her swelled, spiraled open, and became a shining white flower. The bloom was like none she'd seen before. Its fragrance was warm and smelled of summer. She felt something in her stomach, something alien yet familiar. Melinda surprised herself with a laugh, pure and ringing like a little girl's.

The sound sent echoes and ripples into the air around her, edging the garden in day. There was such sunshine in the sound that the plant before her burst into bloom with audible pops, like little firecrackers. She laughed again, and the pool of silvery light spread, bringing other plants out of the darkness. As she glanced around, each one turned green and burst into bloom.

Her laughter was uncontrollable now. It took on a life of its own, filling her with a joy she had never known. Melinda was happy to follow wherever it led. The pool of silvery light spread quickly with her acceptance. Whatever it touched was renewed. Aromatic herbs sprouted from the dry grass. New leaves, flowers, and fruit sprouted from the trees. The whole world was alive.

And Melinda was alive, too.

When dawn came, she was still laughing. Her sister, Louise, found her in the garden, surrounded by growing things that hadn't been there the night before. Melinda was still in her nightgown and touching everything she passed. Sometimes, she laughed out loud, so that the birds answered her from the trees, and sometimes, quietly to herself, as though she shared a secret with the dewdrops and ladybugs.

Louise was sure she'd gone mad. She took Melinda's hand and pulled her inside. Yet everywhere Melinda went, the rooms of the house seemed lighter, more open, free of the shadows that had collected in the corners and draped over everything like dust.

That day was the most beautiful day anyone in town could remember. That year, spring came a full month early and stayed a month longer, before blending into the heat of summer. Melinda Miller became the heart and soul of the town. She was known always to offer a touch or smile to cheer the sad. She had become a garden that was forever in bloom.

Stephen Kopel

Intruder

You stormed the vestibule

of my heart,

crashing

into accumulations of

minor hurts and major sorrows,

stomping

on my knotted carpet

of recriminations,

pounding

on thin walls

of neglected conscience,

smashing

tear stained

panels,

wiping

up emotional spills

that clogged my one hallway

to happiness.

Of course,

I opened the front door

knowing that the whole house

needs rearranging.

Want the job?

Julie Payne Britton

Mid-Life

I spent a long night away from home,

put up in a farmhouse

on the far side of the Berkshires.

I was among friends but felt

rough and clunky in the darkness.

Separated from my own

pillow case, journal,

and unset clock,

I hardly knew myself.

I grew angry.

Why am I comfortable

only in my own home?

That night, I dreamed of tidal waves,

and searching for high ground.

When daylight broke, I thought,

maybe

this vague torment

is the jitterbug of a new day,

the sunny side of the street

on a frozen afternoon,

the black arrow on a street sign

that just says

turn.

Amira Salaam Amro

November, 1989

He's giving himself an injection. That's all. A shot in the vein. Nothing too strange. Self-medication. It happens all over the United States. Across homes and in public restrooms, men and women shoot themselves in the vein. But he's injecting himself in San Diego, and his parents are visiting, and his father sees him, and he has to tell them everything.

"I'm not a drug addict," he says.

His father does not respond. His dark face is pale. He is looking down and crying.

"Don't cry," Sohrab says. "I can explain."

But his father brushes him away. A push. Sohrab falls back a couple of steps, a couple of steps behind. His father continues to weep, large tears running down his bony cheeks.

His father is older now. He has witnessed the Iranian Revolution and has seen his family's land auctioned off before his eyes. At age nineteen, his dreams crumbled, as he left behind his home, his mother, and his achievements, for a new country that he could not relate to. But he'd never expected to walk in on his son shooting himself in the vein.

"I'm going to tell your mother that we should leave," his father says, still looking at his feet, not wanting to meet his son's gaze.

"No," Sohrab says. "Don't leave. Let me explain."

It's November, 1989. The young man is skinny. His hairline is receding. His father looks at this frail son, the youngest of the ten he's produced. He remembers when this son was born. He's always been frail. The ugly duckling. The last baby. He'd been born with a cleft lip. Now his son has a mustache. How skinny he looks, his father thinks to himself with disgust.

"Mary Ann," the father calls out in a Persian accent. Mary Ann, his wife, is not responding. A whiff of smoke hits his nose, and he knows that she's hiding outside on the balcony with a cigarette. She's been doing this for thirty years now. Thirty long years of her smelling like breath spray, chewing gum, and tobacco. It's better than the drinking, he thinks.

He'd given his wife her first drink as an anti-depressant. He's a doctor. "*Aghayeh* Doctor," people called him out of respect in Iran.

Mary Ann had been depressed when she'd moved to Iran, forty years ago. They'd kept making babies. No contraceptives, of course. She was a devout Catholic. And each time she'd pop another one out, her depression would deepen. More diapers to change. Less attention from him, her Iranian husband who'd brought her to his country to live communally with his mother. Finally they'd moved out of his mother's house. As their own family had grown. As the money came in. As he became less available, and she, more depressed.

Mary Ann used to lock herself up and retreat from the noisiness of the street below. The streets of Tehran were never quiet, even from high up in their large home surrounded by the garden and the gate. She could always hear the cars zooming by, the taxi drivers beeping, the beggars ringing at their door, pleading for food, a crying child in their arms. She'd hide away in her bedroom. Even her own children were always asking for more. More time, more clothes, more games, more food, more love. It was a cycle she hadn't planned for when she'd been a girl living in Staten Island, riding behind her boyfriends on their motorbikes. She often reminisced about them, the handsome Irish boys who used to take her out to nice restaurants.

When she'd met her future husband at the hospital where she was a nurse, she'd known he was different. Ali was exotic and handsome. The nurses had nicknamed him "The Prince." Perhaps he could have been a fleeting relationship or passionate moment. Not so. She got pregnant. They got married. She had borne her first child.

Mary Ann had taken her first drink when Ali had handed it to her.

"This will make you feel better," he'd said.

It had. It had tasted a bit bitter, but had warmed her throat and gone to her head quickly.

When she drank wine, everything was different. She'd speak in a blur, trying hard to enunciate. She'd laugh. She'd want him a bit more. She hated him less when she'd had a couple of drinks. When she drank, she forgot the sins that made her fall to her knees each night to pray for forgiveness. The alcohol eased her guilt over marrying a man who didn't recognize Jesus, over conceiving that first child out of wedlock in his small Brooklyn apartment.

Mary Ann comes down the stairs chewing on her peppermint gum. She is breathing deeply to control the urge to have one more cigarette. Ali knows the signs of her weaknesses.

He'd gotten mad once, very mad, he remembers, when she'd had too much to drink and danced too close to an American sailor stationed in Iran. He'd never seen her dance that close to anybody. Ali himself couldn't remember ever holding her that close. Now, he remembers the anger. As she walks down the stairs, forty years later, he remembers how he had wanted to hit her, and how his six daughters had fallen over their mother to protect her from his beatings. Seeing them hollering over their drunk mother had stopped him from actually touching her. He hadn't wanted to set a bad precedent for them. He didn't want his girls to marry wife beaters.

Mary Ann's six daughters had also had to deal with their mother's alcoholism. The youngest at the time, Firouzeh, had once run up to him when Ali had returned home from work.

"Look what I found," she'd said, holding a shampoo bottle. "I was in Mommy's bathroom. I was going to wash my hair, but this isn't shampoo."

Mary Ann had begun to hide alcohol wherever she could. In shampoo bottles. In flasks under her pillow. In strange containers at the back of the freezer. Her hiding places revealed her secret guilt.

Mary Ann had drunk through her pregnancies. Her excessive drinking throughout Sohrab's pregnancy was, they both thought, the reason he had been born premature and with a cleft lip. But Ali had stopped caring by then. He'd stopped telling her what to do. As the years had passed, he'd felt her disappear behind the addiction, like an animal going into hibernation. They still lived with each other, but in separate rooms, in different wings of the house. She cooked meals for him, but the fish was always tasteless, the chicken bland. Coming up in a few weeks was their fiftieth anniversary.

When Mary Ann arrives at the foot of the stairs, Ali tries to speak. He opens his mouth but swallows his words and sobs.

"What's wrong?" she says.

Sohrab answers. "Mom, I have something to say. I've had to tell you this for too long."

Mary Ann looks back at Ali. He is still speechless. She walks over and hugs him. Tears cover her face too. She doesn't know why she is crying. It has been a while since she's felt Ali so close to her. Ali can smell her minty tobacco breath, and it feels soothing for the first time in years.

Sohrab stands alone. He tries to smile at them, but his face crumples with hysterical sobs. He covers his eyes with one hand and rests the other on the back of the plaid couch. His living room is organized, meticulous even, with furniture collected throughout the decades, handed down to him, the youngest of ten siblings. The baby of the family. The couch is from the seventies. On the side table stand several photographs. One of Mary Ann and Ali when they were young parents. Another picture of the ten children, their smiling faces in order of age and height. Alone on a window sill, stands a photograph in a silver frame. The man is Sohrab's age. He seems surprised by the picture, for he is looking back over his shoulder at the camera. His eyes are an intense blue.

"Why are we all crying?" Mary Ann says. "Can somebody tell me what's going on?"

She's smiling through her tears, hoping that perhaps this melodrama has been staged, one of those bursts of emotion that sometimes occur in order to heal years of pain.

"Mommy, I have AIDS." Sohrab's voice is surprisingly strong.

Ali continues to look down. He didn't need Sohrab to tell him. He's a doctor. He knows that Sohrab wasn't shooting heroine, that it was medicine to keep him alive. He'd recognized the antiretroviral tablets on the table in his son's room. He's seen images of HIV positive men and women, their skin yellow from the medication and covered in Kaposi Sarcoma lesions. The day before, he'd noticed one of those purple sores on Sohrab's neck. He'd said nothing and pushed it from his mind. Seeing Sohrab injecting himself was just confirmation of what he hadn't wanted to admit.

Mary Ann stands tall. She is a woman of strong build and heavy bones, yet she is slim. She is still beautiful. She looks at Sohrab and sees what her husband had seen the day before. She sees the red plaque behind his ear. She sees how much weight he's lost. She sees him as a baby. The last one to come out of her body. She's always felt sorry for him. She's always felt guilty for having drunk so much during that last pregnancy.

He was always the sweet one, the one who had jokes to tell, the creative one who drew sketches of cars and listened to sad songs on the radio. He would often crawl into bed with his parents, when they'd still shared a bed. He'd sleep between them, soothed by his father's snoring.

Mary Ann has heard about AIDS. In church they'd spoken about it. It was hitting like an epidemic, and it was killing homosexuals. "No," she thinks, "it can't be."

"I'm on medication," Sohrab continues, as though reading from a script. His voice sounds almost robotic. "I'm still okay, but it's painful. I didn't want to upset you, so I kept it from you. The other kids know though."

Ali's head feels heavier than ever. He still can't look Sohrab in the eye.

Sohrab picks up the picture of the man with the intense blue eyes.

"This is Trevor." His lips quiver as he says these words. Memories of his lost lover flood his mind. He can feel the weight of the truth he is finally sharing with his parents. "He died three years ago."

Ali walks toward the door and leaves the apartment. He walks to the elevator and presses the button to descend. The elevator drops quickly. He finds himself alone on the street. It's a busy street. Sohrab lives in the artsy section of town. The neighborhood is strange to Ali. It's too industrial, too dirty, and too busy. He glances up at his son's building and walks northward. He has the sensation that there is no pavement beneath his feet. The sun is shining, but Ali wishes it wasn't. He has always associated sunny days with happy moments. He walks rapidly. He continues his pace for an hour perhaps, beating a straight path along Woodburn Avenue. He stops in front of a coffee shop without knowing why.

The coffee shop is one of those diner-like places from the fifties. It has framed Coca-Cola advertisements and a bar with stools. Ali sits at the bar and orders a vanilla milkshake. He remembers when he'd first arrived in the United States, an immigrant with a few Iranian *tomans* in his pocket. He'd been accepted by Columbia University. He'd left behind his father who cuckolded his mother with the maids, his mother with her constant complaints, and his unmarried sister. He was intent on making something of his life. He'd never go back to Iran, he'd decided when he'd first arrived in America. He'd changed his family name to cut all ties to his ancestors. He'd planned to make a new life for himself.

He'd married an American woman, but somehow circumstances had brought him back to Iran, and then back again to the States, like a boomerang. He no longer knows where he'd wanted to end up in the first place. All he knows is that his son is dying and that he has not slept beside his wife for over a decade.

The milkshake soothes his throat. Mary Ann used to make milkshakes for him. She'd made them in Iran and impressed their guests. He orders another one and drinks it as quickly. He can feel his stomach filling up, and he is nauseated. Still, he finishes it. He walks into the men's room and splashes cold water on his face. Then, he walks out of the coffee shop and back onto Woodburn Avenue, toward his son's apartment.

He thinks of the afternoon ahead. He'll call the travel agent and ask her to extend their stay. He and Mary Ann will sit down with Sohrab and discuss things. They'll have to meet with his doctor. Tonight he wants to share his wife's bed. He wants to hold her tightly.

Bill Roberts

Curtain Call

When you've been a performer onstage,

you realize just how difficult it is for a fellow

entertainer to get up there, heavily made up,

perhaps in a wig and cumbersome costume,

to open his mouth wide, and sing with gusto.

To do this flawlessly, not missing a cue, a note,

a glance at his leading lady, and pull it all off

to near perfection deserves a heart-felt Bravo!

and standing ovation, well deserved accolades

that you yourself probably never received.

It's okay, you say. I understand. And you do.

You were not trained in opera. If only you'd had

the gift of a fine tenor or baritone, how sweet

it would have been to be Alfredo in *Traviata* or

the Duke of Mantua, or Siegfried for Wagner.

So when you see an inspired performance

in a difficult role, by one so highly trained

and yet so deftly restrained, stand on your feet

and applaud till your hands hurt, allowing tears

to stream freely down your cheeks.

Yell Bravo! to the brave fellow so overcome

with emotion from his role that he reels as he bows,

touches his heart, throws kisses to one and all of us,

feeling perhaps that he plays us at our finest,

though never before to such an adoring audience.

Almost Spring

"Would you rather be attractive or pretty?"

Sally paused, panicked as she always was whenever anybody asked her a direct question. From the tone of the question, she could tell Helen had already made up her mind. Her query was less a prelude to discussion than a test, like the riddle of the Sphinx, or a pretext for Helen to parade the virtues of her own opinion, whatever that might turn out to be. Pretending to consider, Sally scrunched up her face.

"Pretty," she ventured.

Helen smiled, looking smug. Sally knew she'd blundered.

"Interesting," Helen said.

"Why, what do you think?"

"I'd so much rather be attractive. Pretty is boring, and it doesn't last. If you're attractive, you're always attractive."

Helen was attractive, Sally thought, with her red-brown hair, brown eyes, and lightly freckled nose. Her decisiveness. Her certainty.

"You're attractive," she said aloud. Vaguely, she realized that this was what Helen had been fishing for, and that, therefore, she probably shouldn't have said it.

"Ugh, I'm fat. I have to go on a diet. Look at this flab." Helen slapped at her belly in disgust.

The girls lay sprawled, Helen on the bed, Sally on the floor of Helen's bedroom. Soon, they would both turn sixteen — Sally in May, Helen in July. They had known each other since childhood and had been best friends for two years now. They were forever weathering personal crises and trading opinions on top ten songs, parental injustices, teachers, classmates, boys, as well as the "current events" frequently discussed in social studies classes at their large, rather liberal, suburban high school.

"You're not fat," Sally said, feeling obliged.

"Yes, I am. I need to lose ten pounds."

"So do I." Sally sighed, envisioning the blubbery roll across her abdomen. How would she hide it in a bathing suit? She would have to eat less, which would lead to another round of arguments with her mother. Helen had not disagreed with her. That must mean she looked really awful. In her mind's eye, her belly grew larger, dead white, dimpled and tumescent, a parasitic excrescence. No matter how little she ate, she would never entirely get rid of it. Sally felt suddenly exhausted.

Helen hadn't said she was attractive, either. Sally had little sense of how she looked.

She wanted to jump up and examine her reflection in the mirror, as she did at home, but of course she couldn't. Not now, not here. She stiffened with the effort of suppressing the impulse.

So recently, it had not mattered. As a child, Sally had only cared to be comfortable. She had detested holidays, when her mother insisted on dressing her in stiff, scratchy petticoats, embroidered blouses, and velvet skirts; in tights or little cuffed socks, and patent leather shoes with straps. In the dress-up clothes, she had felt vulnerable, pinned down, reduced, as she felt now in her body. Then, she had fumed when grownups cooed and called her "cute."

"What have I got to do with 'cute'?" she might have said, if she could have shaped her emotions into words. What had she to do with "she," after all? She felt neither he nor she. In her mind, she could shift her shape at will, becoming any animal. She ranged with the dinosaurs. She explored the bottom of the sea. At other times she flew.

And now, here she was. Still invisible and vast. More bewildered than ever to find herself nailed by a look or a phrase to that body which she could only see in reflection.

"Your ears are weird," Carla Morelli had noted one day at lunchtime. Half the table had sniggered.

Another time, an officious Angie Fishman had advised, "You shouldn't wear short skirts. You have heavy thighs."

Driven to the mirror by such remarks, Sally would scrutinize her image for defects, wondering how she could possibly catch and disguise them all. Then again, when she was undressing alone at bedtime, in the light of a single lamp, Sally would stand naked before the glass and think that maybe she looked all right. Maybe she was even pretty. Always, there remained a vestige of her former nobility, an indifference to appearances, so that the figure before her never seemed to be herself, but rather, a demanding twin with whom she found herself confused.

"I'm changing this blouse," Helen announced, rolling off her bed. She went over to her bureau and opened a drawer.

"Where's that shirt? If my sister has it, I'll kill her. I thought it was here. She always takes my things. Sa-rah? *Sarah!*"

Sally listened, a bit embarrassed, as she always was by the claustrophobic interactions between Helen and her sister. She herself was an only child.

If Sarah heard Helen's call, she didn't respond. Helen opened another drawer, rummaging.

"I'll kill her if — Oh. Here it is!"

Somewhat sheepishly, Helen extracted a tee shirt with an image of a castle silk-screened onto the front.

"I love tee shirts. Don't you?"

"Yeah."

Helen held up the shirt for general admiration, and then began to unbutton her blouse.

Sally had lost her childhood resistance to clothes. Formerly a betrayal, dressing had become an extension of that protean invisibility of her younger self, a mode of both expression and disguise. Yet whereas childhood's fantastic permutations had been effortless, clothes were an endless source of anxiety and expense. You had to work at clothes. You had to have certain jeans, certain shoes, and a particular style of skirt. Sometimes, you thought you had the correct look, only to discover some detail of fabric or stitching that made it wrong. You couldn't be seen in it then. You had to endure it all. Your disappointment, your mother's uncomprehending irritation, and your guilt at wasting her money. Again, you waited for your mother to buy you the real thing, the right thing. Only by then, it wasn't right. It was wrong, and there was something else you had to have.

Sally thought wistfully of the girls who were somehow always right, and of the boys who would speak only to them. They all smoked cigarettes, and their jeans were the blue of the sea glimpsed from far away.

"How do I look?" Helen asked.

"You look great."

Helen gazed out the window.

"Let's go for a walk."

"Yeah, let's."

Sally hefted herself up off the floor. She wanted the streets and the brisk air, yet she felt reluctant to leave the comfort of Helen's attic with its luxuriant disorder, its posters and pots of Swedish ivy. It was so different from her cramped room at home, which Sally felt to be only conditionally hers, subject at all times to invasion by her mother. Helen's mother never ventured into her daughter's domain. She limited herself to a call from downstairs that announced a departure or a meal, or occasionally, a cautious inquiry from the threshold.

The girls pulled on their shoes and coats and clattered down the stairs.

"Sally and I are going for a walk!" Helen yelled.

"Okay, dear," came the reply, from somewhere in the vicinity of the kitchen, as if it were the voice of the house itself.

Outside, wind buffeted them. It was one of those days in March when spring seems far away. Blood rose in Sally's cheeks. She shoved her hands into her pockets and bent forward. Helen danced ahead with her characteristic bravado, jacket open and scarf flapping.

"I love walks," she crowed, twirling theatrically.

"Me too."

"But as soon as I'm sixteen, I'm gonna get my license."

"I can't wait."

They took a familiar path down quiet streets lined with big Victorian and neo-Colonial houses. On this blustery afternoon, no one else was out. Nevertheless, as the girls approached a certain corner, Sally felt her chest tighten.

"Remember that day we saw him?" Helen said predictably, with a smirk.

"Who?" Sally affected ignorance.

"You know. Peach Pit."

"Oh yeah. That was funny." Sally laughed, as if she felt no pain.

"I think he saw us."

"What a jerk."

"Peach Pit," Helen's nickname for Sally's first and only boyfriend, Rick Gardiner, was one of the artifacts of their intimacy.

The name was part of the code, developed over the course of countless lazy afternoons and giggly sleepover dates, that separated them from others and made them best friends. "Peach Pit," Helen would intone mysteriously at lunch in the school cafeteria, sending them both into paroxysms of laughter, while other lesser cronies would sit stony-faced, incognizant and unmoved.

"Everyone was so shocked when you started going out with him. But it was because you were the first. You broke away from the clique."

"Yeah." In effect it was true, and yet Sally could not wholeheartedly accept Helen's assessment of her behavior as having been deliberate and brave. She felt vaguely ashamed, as if she were decorated with an honor she did not deserve. Was it brave for one dying of thirst to cross burning stones for water? And what if there was no water after all, but only a mirage?

It had not turned out as she had hoped. She had felt shy and scarcely able to speak to him. It was hard to believe that he, an older boy, had noticed her. Voiceless, she had thrown herself into kisses. They were a novel pleasure of which she could scarcely get enough. In the corridors at school she had draped herself around him, defying the disapproval of her friends and the potential horror of her mother. Finally, alone with him in his room on a Saturday afternoon, she had taken off her blouse and jeans and sat on the edge of the bed in her underwear, while he, surveying her body approvingly, said, "You're a piece."

She did not know other boys. She had no brothers, and her father was taciturn, spending evenings behind the newspaper. She had heard that they only wanted one thing. Probably it was true. Still, she was dismayed when Rick ogled other girls.

"That girl is stacked," he would say, of someone she disliked.

"She's not a nice person."

"I didn't say she was nice. I said she was stacked. Besides, she doesn't seem so bad to me."

"You haven't seen the other side of her."

"I've seen both sides. The right and the left."

Versed in the idiom of romances and fairy tales, Sally could not speak of those sessions in his room. She could not speak of them, for surely it was all taboo — his muscular, half-naked body; the feel of his hands on her skin; and her dizzy delight. He smelled of medicinal soap. As they lay entwined on his bed, Sally glimpsed the lush, green leaves and lawns of June through the Venetian blinds. The foliage seemed suspended in an amber luminosity, and yet the hours spent with Rick passed and were gone. The shadows lengthened. She would always go home.

Sally could speak even less of the disbelieving pain during those weeks when he first ceased to call. She had no right to grieve openly over what had been a forbidden indulgence. School was out for the summer, and he lived on the opposite side of town. There would be no opportunities to run into him until the fall.

"You're not chasing after that boy," her mother had ordered. "You don't call." Still, one day when her mother had gone out to the store, Sally had called, choking on her anxiety when one of his brothers answered.

"May I please speak to Rick," she had asked, in almost a whisper.

Nothing could have prepared her for the disinterest in his tone, the invitation that did not come, the answer to a question she did not dare to ask.

He had spoken enthusiastically of a friend of hers. "That girl has it all. She could have guys at her feet."

That summer, Sally took to walking. She did own a bicycle, a venerable three-speed, which she usually rode in the company of friends who owned racing bikes. She enjoyed the wind in her hair and the sorties into exotic and unfamiliar neighborhoods. Once at twilight, she'd sailed past a garden in which she'd glimpsed flowers like balls of stars floating atop tall stalks. They were so strange, like an image in a dream. When she'd returned a week later, the flowers had gone to seed, and stood, mere skeletons.

Yet, Sally preferred to walk. This may have been because she stored her bicycle in the basement of their apartment building. If her father were off at work, as he usually was, she would have to call upon her mother to carry it up the steep steps. Sally hated to watch her struggle, red-faced and breathless, amidst the tangle of handlebars, pedals, and crazily spinning wheels.

Sally had walked with the hope, however remote, that she might run into Rick. She never dared to stroll down his street, but whenever she neared its vicinity, she kept a lookout for the dark blue Buick that he drove. It belonged to his parents. Once, fantastically, she had seen him behind the wheel. As he passed, he'd stared and honked the horn. But Sally had been with Helen, and so, affected indifference.

Now, Rick hardly mattered. She no longer walked in quest of him, but of Long Island Sound. More and more, it seemed she could not bear the confines of her room at home, its door shut against the roar of her mother's vacuum cleaner. Propelled by her own desperation, she would stride along the busy avenues, down sidewalks studded with dog stool and discarded fast-food wraps, until she found herself in a more gracious part of town. There, the houses were huge and silent, as if under an enchantment. Only occasionally did Sally hear the throb of rock music emanating from some teenager's bedroom. At last, she would round a bend in the road, and there it would be. The seawall, and beyond it, the beach.

Sometimes, she brought her diary or a sketchbook, but she grew to dread the inquiries, however infrequent, of nosy strangers. For the most part, nowadays, she sat on a bench or a rock, staring out over the Sound, with the cries of the seagulls echoing around her.

"You were the first," she heard Helen repeat. "You were right. You had to break out of the clique."

Now, they were here, at the beach. The wind blew, lashing Sally's hair across her face and into her mouth. Her eyes filled with tears. She strained against the wind, sand shifting beneath her feet. To their right lay the harbor with its moored boats rocking. In front of them, the jetty pointed like an arrow or a finger.

Helen swooped and swirled. She was always in motion. Trudging next to her, Sally felt like a lump. Now, Helen broke away, running towards the water. Her arms spread like wings. Sally followed her, pushing with all of her strength against the wind.

It seemed that Helen would take off and fly. She climbed easily up onto the jetty. Sally continued in her wake, balancing precariously on the uneven boulders. They were slippery and stained with seagull droppings. To either side, waves slapped, stirring the seaweed that fanned outward from the rocks.

Helen had come to a halt a few yards ahead, at the very tip of the jetty. Affecting a romantic pose, she stood with her hair billowing out behind her. She was watching something. Sally searched the distance. All at once, with a catch of her breath, she saw what Helen saw. A sailboat. Gliding on waves and wind, it looked ineffably serene. It appeared to be voyaging to some distant, blessed city built of golden stone, where birds sang in gardens and children, in clothing the color of jewels, danced around the fountains in the squares.

But it was Helen's sailboat and Helen's city. She had claimed them. Leave it to Helen to stake out the best view. Sally turned bitterly away toward the harbor, and then stopped mid-stride.

Just above the horizon, the sun hung suspended. Sally stared into its light, feeling the blazing warmth upon her face, feeling herself and everything around her. The harbor and the jetty, Helen and her sailboat, the beach, and the Sound were growing radiant and ethereal, as if transmuted into light.

"Sally!" Helen was calling. "Sally!"

It was hard to look away. Finally, Sally turned. Helen stood, regarding her.

"Sally! You look so beautiful, standing there."

Barry Ballard

The Silent Errand of Anything

There is a distraction in this hour

that can be anything: the ordinary

exposed shadows,

the weight of truth

waking up out of them,

or the long day's body of memory

surviving the sour

borders of artificial light.

It carries warnings that you'll see

yourself, through the gaping holes

of your armor, or your ceremonies.

It will leave you as the same person,

occupying the same space,

and your mind,

opened by the inward gaze,

begins its silent errand,

writing and unwriting, condemning

the hardships, or learning how to forgive.

Kate Niles

Down Below

Silence. Me and Ricky lie by ourselves in our basement bedroom, the first room we've had to share in our whole life. We don't get why this has to be the case, but when they bought the house, Mom and Dad were full of the big basement and how we could have the run of it. Problem is, it's not finished, and the black widows own it. There's two perfectly good rooms upstairs, but Mom wants both of them. Kind of piggy of her, though if we ask to move upstairs, we're the ones who're called piggy.

Over on his bed, Ricky's scowling. I decide he doesn't want to be pestered, so I don't try to talk to him. It's a cold October, and we're still getting used to the new school. We moved here in June. It's the fourth time we've moved, and I'm only ten.

We sit here with our noses in books, until we hear Mom on the stairs, moving toward the laundry. When she comes in with a full clothes basket, Ricky leaves, and I finally ask why we move so much. I have to ask quick, because I know she'll only stay long enough to sort our clothes, not hers and Dad's, and then go back upstairs.

It scares me a little to ask. You never know about Mom. She might be okay with a question, or she might think I'm complaining, when all I want is to know something. This time, though, Mom laughs and jokes that she and Dad are itinerant professors, Tom Joads of the academic world. It's been tough for the past few years, she says. Since 1970, when the Ph.D. market dried up.

"What's Tom Joad?" I ask. Ricky's gone to the den and has the TV on, so I have to speak up a little. I've heard all about Ph.D.s but not about Tom Joad.

"*Who* is Tom Joad. Who, you mean. He's a character in John Steinbeck's *The Grapes of Wrath*. It's a novel about people moving west in the Depression."

"You mean kind of like Dad's family?"

Mom's eyes waver at me, the way they do when she's not sure she wants to admit to something. I sink a little inside. Her mood shifts so quick sometimes. She snaps a shirt. "Sort of. Only the Graves weren't Okies. They were from Nebraska. And they were better educated."

"Oh." I decide not to talk anymore.

Who is Tom Joad. I can never say anything without some correction coming. Who is Tom Joad. I think about the next time I'll visit the library. I'll read a little, sitting there on the floor with the book open, blocking the aisle so that people have to step over me. I'll learn who Tom Joad is, and then put the book back on the shelves. I might think about checking it out, but it'll probably look too big and hard, and so I'll skip to my favorites — Nancy Drew, Laura Ingalls Wilder, biographies for kids.

This town's got a good library. This is the third Rocky Mountain town we've lived in. I love the Rockies. We just did a unit in school on Chief Ouray and the Utes, and I pretend I'm an Ute girl half the time now. The first town, where I was born, was in the South, but Mom and Dad only lived there a year, and I don't remember any of it. I was too young to read books then, anyway.

When Mom's done with the laundry and disappears upstairs, I'm left with the concrete and spiders. The black widows rule the corners. Me and Ricky hate to admit it, but we're afraid of stepping on them at night. Dad sprays, but it doesn't do much good. He holds a metal can in one hand and a stiff hose-like thing in the other, and puts this nasty-smelling stuff all over the place.

Outside our door is a hall. To the right, the stairs go up, and past that, it opens into the garage, where Dad's got his workbenches and tools. He has this brown board full of holes in it that he hangs on the wall. He hangs hooks in the holes and his tools on the hooks. He's very picky about his tools and tells us never to touch them. When he's making something — bookshelves, mostly, because both Mom and him have a ton of books — he's very concentrated and tight. Like a spring wound up. His biceps bulge and his T-shirt stretches across his back so you can see his muscles working, and he holds his mouth as if the rows of his teeth are two parts of a puzzle snapped together.

I want him to stop being so wound up. Jaw so tight. What makes him happy is not Mom or Ricky or our house. But it might be me, if I can just be like one of his students he hangs around with so much. Sometimes, when it's just us two, I can make his eyes brighten the way they do when Ike or Peter come visit, or the way they did in the last place we lived, with his students then — Steve Rye and Doug Wilson. I do this — make him light up — by cracking a joke like the ones they crack. ("Dad, why did the cowboy buy a dachshund?" "Why?" "Because he was told to get a long little doggie!") And then he'll laugh, tipping his head back, so that his thin lips stretch, and soon, all I see are small rows of teeth, like piano keys, and his chin jutting out. Then he brings his head down, and the moment's over. But it's enough. It's enough to let me know that if I just work it right, I can win his heart as much as any of those boys he teaches.

The black widows give us an idea.

"Let's make a web," Ricky says.

"A spider web?"

"Duh. What other kind?"

"Thought you hated widows." I poked one once, so it would roll over and I could show him the red hourglass on its belly. He about had a heart attack.

"I didn't say a widow web. Just a general web."

"Okay," I say, and we seem to know exactly what we're both talking about, even though we haven't talked about it at all. Upstairs, we take some string from the gift-wrapping drawer, also scissors and tape. We go back down and start in the corner opposite the door, then pull a string in from all the other corners. Four Corners. Just like the monument not that far from here, a couple of hours, where me and Ricky and Dad stopped on a trip once this past summer. Mom doesn't like camping or driving very much, so in the summers we go places without her. This is another way to make Dad almost happy. Go out with him, like he does with his students, and joke around outside. He doesn't ever take us backpacking (the real way to be in the wilderness), but he will take us to see national parks and go camping.

I loved visiting the Four Corners Monument. You could have a foot in Utah and Arizona at the same time, put your hands down to cover

New Mexico and Colorado. Kind of like State Twister. And if you lifted your head, you could see in all directions, the red desert going on forever, all bluffs and sun. A few Navajos set up ramadas nearby, selling earrings and fry bread and Cokes, but other than that, there's just some Port-a-Potties squatting out in the sun and the road in. Way out, middle of nowhere. An X made up for no reason. A cross in the sand. No rivers or mountain ranges showed that there should be four states meeting there, but there they were. As if somebody-or-other explorer type played God one day, pointed a finger, and drew the lines out. Crazy.

I pull the Arizona string in from the corner in that direction, southwest. Ricky runs in the New Mexico one, from southeast. He holds the two together in the center, while I tack Utah to the corner and walk toward Ricky. Finally, Colorado. The one by the door, the state where we are, the one I want all of a sudden, stronger than any other line. I can't say why, except my heart's going a hundred miles a minute, and I feel the way Mom acts when a truck passes us on the highway, and she freaks out. I hate feeling this way. I hate being a wimp like her. But still, I wish that string were thick as a ski tow, or better yet, see-through but really strong, like fishing wire. Yeah, that's good, fishing wire.

Ricky ties the states together. Now we have our own Four Corners Monument in the middle of the room. Five feet high, maybe, as high as Ricky's arms will reach, halfway between the light on the ceiling and the concrete floor.

But the four strings by themselves will not stop a thing. So we let the Monument droop while we weave strings around and around, spiders making our nest. What was that Greek goddess spider? Ariadne? Was that it? Are we Ariadne? Or Spider Woman, like the Navajo have. I think Spider Woman is better. I mean, the Navajo Reservation spills into three of the Four Corners states. But does Spider Woman weave? Mrs. Lovato at school seems to think she just warns the Hero Twins about their father. That's good, but mainly, I want Spider Woman to weave; she has to weave — she's a spider. I wonder if the Utes have Spider Woman too. The Utes ran around all these states as well. I love Indians, and it's important to know who all and what all went on in the place where I live.

We create a new world in our room. Once the web is up we put a stick up in the middle to make it all taut. The room now has the gray cement walls, the two kids' beds under the web, across and zigzag from each other, and the white web. That's all there is.

CONTRIBUTORS' NOTES

AMIRA SALAAM AMRO is a retired lawyer. She lives in New York City with her husband Dean and is dedicating her time to writing.

BARRY BALLARD'S poetry has recently appeared in the *Evansville Review*, *Blue Mesa*, *Louisiana Literature*, and the *Florida Review*. His collection *First Probe to Antarctica* won the Bright Hill Press Award in 2001. His latest book of poetry, *Plowing to the End of the Road*, was nominated for a Pushcart Prize and won the Finishing Line Press Award in 2002.

JULIE PAYNE BRITTON received an Honorable Award from the 2002 New England Writer's Conference. She is currently writing a memoir of her mother's life entitled *A Daughter's Lament*.

SAMANTHA HOLLOWAY'S fiction has recently appeared in the *Flagler Review*, and *Phoenix*. She served on the editorial board of *Arete* for a year. Her writing is inspired by her travels through Turkey, Italy, and Japan.

STEPHEN KOPEL is known as San Francisco's "pedaling poet." He is the author of two collections of poetry, *Crux* (Calliope Press, 2001) and *Spritz* (Regent Press, 2003). *Spritz* was nominated for Pushcart Prize XXV. Mr. Kopel is also the creator of the Word Painters poetry event. His work has appeared in more than 220 literary journals.

KATE NILES was the recipient of the Colorado Council of the Arts Individual Artist Fellowship for Creative Writing in 2003. This piece is excerpted from her first novel, *The Basket Maker* (GreyCore Press, 2004), a finalist in the Heekin Group Foundation Awards for a novel-in-progress, and now nominated for the Mountains/Plains Book Association Book of the Year Award. Her book of poems, *Geographies of the Heart*, was published by Blue Heron Press in 1997. Her poetry, short stories, and essays have appeared in literary journals and have been broadcast on public radio.

BILL ROBERTS' work was recently published by *Parnassus Literary Review*, *HazMat Review*, *Wavelength*, and *Spare Change News*. He is a semi-retired scientist who works at the infamous Lab at Los Alamos. If he could turn the clock back and conjure up sufficient talent, he would have become a ballet dancer.

NITA SEMBROWICH'S fiction was recently published in *Eclectica*. She has been writing all her life, in a variety of forms and genres. She is currently studying landscape design at the Landscape Institute of the Arnold Arboretum. She lives in Cambridge, Massachusetts.

*The journal is offered in love
to the eternal presence of
Maharishi Mahesh Yogi.*

May we all live in peace together.

There is no end,
for there is no beginning.

SUBSCRIBE

Lalitamba
P.O. Box; 131
Planetarium Station
New York, NY 10024

_____$10 One-year subscribtion (one issue)

_____$19 Two-year subscription (two issues)

Please add $4.95 for postage and handling, and enclose a check written to *Lalitamba*.

Begin my subscription with issue number _____

Name_____

Address_____

City, State, Zip_____

Please send a gift subscription to:

Name_____

Address_____

City, State, Zip_____

SUPPORT REFUGE

Refuge is a crisis center committed to supporting homeless women in New York City.

Years ago, our director was a magazine journalist. She traveled the world to speak with the managers of venerable hotels, as well as acclaimed chefs and restaurateurs. It is their standards in hospitality and service that we look to in serving New York City's homeless. At the same time, we've seen that loving connection is more important than anything material.

Through years of working with people in need of permanent housing, we understand how stressful the situation can be. It is not unusual for someone to be "in the system" for two years before finally receiving housing. During this time, people may be shuttled from one shelter to another, without feeling that they belong anywhere.

Refuge is a bed-and-breakfast style facility that feels like home. We welcome everyone who stays here with warmth and respect. Guests cozy up to watch films, enjoy an extensive book and music library, and find peace of mind in the meditation sanctuary. We also offer support groups and cultural programs, as well as a personal mentoring program to encourage our women to be all that they can be.

One of our mentors often spoke about how powerful the kindness of strangers could be. Kindness is the way to see each other through the rough times and back home to the heart. We are one human family. This is a basic truth upon which Refuge was founded.

Refuge is in partnership with *Lalitamba*.

To make a tax-deductible donation to Refuge, please send a check to Lalitamba-Refuge at P.O. Box 131, Planetarium Station, New York, NY 10024. Thank you!

www.threejewelsrefuge.org